OTHELLO

William Shakespeare

AUTHORED by Michelle Rosenberg
UPDATED AND REVISED by Gemma Cooper-Novack

COVER DESIGN by Table XI Partners LLC
COVER PHOTO by Olivia Verma and © 2005 GradeSaver, LLC

BOOK DESIGN by Table XI Partners LLC

Published by GradeSaver LLC, www.gradesaver.com

First published in the United States of America by GradeSaver LLC. 2014

GRADESAVER, the GradeSaver logo and the phrase "Getting you the grade since 1999" are registered trademarks of GradeSaver, LLC

ISBN 978-1-60259-412-8

Printed in the United States of America

For other products and additional information please visit
http://www.gradesaver.com

Table of Contents

Table of Contents

Table of Contents

Table of Contents

Teaching Guide - About the Author

William Shakespeare is arguably the most famous writer of the English language, known for both his plays and his sonnets. Though much about his life remains open to debate because of incomplete evidence, the following biography consolidates the most widely-accepted facts of Shakespeare's life and career.

In the mid-sixteenth century, William Shakespeare's father, John Shakespeare, moved to the idyllic town of Stratford-upon-Avon. There, he became a successful landowner, moneylender, glove-maker, and dealer of wool and agricultural goods. In 1557, he married Mary Arden.

During John Shakespeare's time, the British middle class was expanding in both size and wealth, which allowed its members more freedoms and luxuries, as well as a stronger collective voice in local government. John took advantage of the changing times and became a member of the Stratford Council in 1557, which marked the beginning of his illustrious political career. By 1567, he had become bailiff—the highest elected office in Stratford and the equivalent of a modern-day mayor.

William Shakespeare's exact birth date is unknown, but legend pins it on April 23, 1564. Little is known about his childhood, although it is assumed that he attended the local grammar school, the King's New School. The school was staffed by Oxford-educated faculty who taught the students mathematics, natural sciences, logic, Christian ethics, and classical languages and literature.

Shakespeare did not attend university, which was not unusual for the time. The numerous classical and literary references in Shakespeare's plays are a testament, however, to the excellent education he received in grammar school, and speaks to his ability as an autodidact. His early plays, in particular, draw on the works of Seneca and Plautus, and his vocabulary exceeds that of any other English writer of his time by a wide margin.

In 1582, at the age of eighteen, William Shakespeare married twenty-six-year-old Anne Hathaway. They had three children, one of whom died at age 11—by this time, Shakespeare was already a successful playwright. Around 1589, he wrote *Henry VI, Part 1*, which is considered to be his first play. Sometime between 1582 and 1589, Shakespeare moved to London, where he pursued a career as a playwright and actor.

Little information exists about Shakespeare's life as a young playwright in London. Legend characterizes him as a roguish young man who was once forced to flee the city under dubious circumstances, perhaps having to do with his extramarital affairs, but no written sources confirm this facet of his personality. The earliest written record of Shakespeare's life in London comes from a statement by his rival playwright Robert Greene. In *Groatsworth of Witte* (1592), Greene calls Shakespeare an "upstart crow...[who] supposes he is as well able to bombast out a blank verse as the best of you." While this is hardly high praise, it does suggest that Shakespeare rattled London's theatrical hierarchy from the beginning of his career.

With *Richard III, Henry VI, The Comedy of Errors*, and *Titus Andronicus* under his belt, Shakespeare was an accomplished playwright by 1590.* The year 1593, however, marked a major leap forward in his career when he secured a prominent patron, The Earl of Southampton. In addition, *Venus and Adonis* was published; it was one of the first of Shakespeare's known works to be printed, and it was a huge success. By this time, Shakespeare had also made his mark as a poet, as most scholars agree that he wrote the majority of his sonnets in the 1590s.

In 1594, Shakespeare returned to the stage and became a charter member of the Lord Chamberlain's Men (later known as The King's Men). By 1598, Shakespeare had been appointed the "principal comedian" for the troupe; by 1603, he was "principal tragedian." He remained associated with the organization until his death. Although acting and playwriting were not considered noble professions at the time, successful and prosperous actors were relatively well respected. Shakespeare's success left him with a fair amount of money, which he invested in Stratford real estate. He purchased the second-largest house in Stratford for his parents and applied for a coat of arms for his family. His daughters made "good matches," and married wealthy men.

The same year that he joined the Lord Chamberlain's Men, Shakespeare wrote *Romeo and Juliet, Love's Labour's Lost, The Taming of the Shrew*, and several other plays. In 1600, he wrote *Hamlet* and *Julius Caesar*. The first decade of the seventeenth century witnessed the debut performances of many of Shakespeare's most celebrated works, including *Othello* in 1604 or 1605, *Antony and Cleopatra* in 1606 or 1607, and *King Lear* in 1608. The last of Shakespeare's plays to be performed during his lifetime was most likely *King Henry VIII*, in either 1612 or 1613.

William Shakespeare died in 1616 and was buried in the chancel of his church at Stratford.

*The dates of composition and performance of almost all of Shakespeare's plays remain uncertain. The dates used in this note are widely agreed upon by scholars, but there is still significant debate.

Teaching Guide - Study Objectives

If all of the elements of this lesson plan are employed, students will develop the following powers, skills, and understanding:

1. Develop a thorough understanding of the historical and cultural context in which *Othello* was written and apply its themes to contemporary life

2. Read and analyze Shakespeare's writing closely, paying particular attention to his use of figurative language and extended metaphors

3. Analyze and discuss, both individually and as a class, the important and common themes in the play

4. Speak and write insightfully about the ideas contained in *Othello*, including what the students' own opinions are about those ideas

5. Understand the unique aspects of drama as a literary genre

Teaching Guide - Common Core Standards

- 11-12 - CCSS.ELA-Literacy.CCRA.L.4: Determine or clarify the meaning of unknown and multiple-meaning words and phrases by using context clues, analyzing meaningful word parts, and consulting general and specialized reference materials, as appropriate.

- 11-12 - CCSS.ELA-Literacy.CCRA.L.5: Demonstrate understanding of figurative language, word relationships, and nuances in word meanings.

- 11-12 - CCSS.ELA-Literacy.CCRA.R.1: Read closely to determine what the text says explicitly and to make logical inferences from it; cite specific textual evidence when writing or speaking to support conclusions drawn from the text.

- 11-12 - CCSS.ELA-Literacy.CCRA.R.3: Analyze how and why individuals, events, or ideas develop and interact over the course of a text.

- 11-12 - CCSS.ELA-Literacy.CCRA.R.4: Interpret words and phrases as they are used in a text, including determining technical, connotative, and figurative meanings, and analyze how specific word choices shape meaning or tone.

- 11-12 - CCSS.ELA-Literacy.CCRA.R.5: Analyze the structure of texts, including how specific sentences, paragraphs, and larger portions of the text (e.g., a section, chapter, scene, or stanza) relate to each other and the whole.

- 11-12 - CCSS.ELA-Literacy.CCRA.R.6: Assess how point of view or purpose shapes the content and style of a text.

- 11-12 - CCSS.ELA-Literacy.CCRA.R.7: Integrate and evaluate content presented in diverse media and formats, including visually and quantitatively, as well as in words.

- 11-12 - CCSS.ELA-Literacy.CCRA.R.9: Analyze how two or more texts address similar themes or topics in order to build knowledge or to compare the approaches the authors take.

- 11-12 - CCSS.ELA-Literacy.CCRA.W.3: Write narratives to develop real or imagined experiences or events using effective technique, well-chosen details and well-structured event sequences.

- 11-12 - CCSS.ELA-Literacy.CCRA.W.4: Produce clear and coherent writing in which the development, organization, and style are appropriate to task, purpose, and audience.

- 11-12 - CCSS.ELA-Literacy.CCRA.W.6: Use technology, including the Internet, to produce and publish writing and to interact and collaborate with others.

- 11-12 - CCSS.ELA-Literacy.CCRA.W.9: Draw evidence from literary or informational texts to support analysis, reflection, and research.

- 11-12 - CCSS.ELA-Literacy.CCRA.W.10: Write routinely over extended time frames (time for research, reflection, and revision) and shorter time frames (a single sitting or a day or two) for a range of tasks, purposes, and audiences.

- 11-12 - CCSS.ELA-Literacy.CCRA.SL.1: Prepare for and participate effectively in a range of conversations and collaborations with diverse partners, building on others' ideas and expressing their own clearly and persuasively.

- 11-12 - CCSS.ELA-Literacy.CCRA.SL.6: Adapt speech to a variety of contexts and communicative tasks, demonstrating command of formal English when indicated or appropriate.

Teaching Guide - Introduction to Othello

Othello was written by William Shakespeare between 1601 and 1604, and first published in 1622. It is based on an Italian short story called "Un Capitano Moro" ("A Moorish Captain") written by Cinthio and published in 1565.

Othello is one of Shakespeare's most popular tragedies. It explores themes of race, love, betrayal, and loyalty, and is largely a study of human nature and psychology. The play is set during a war between Venice and the Ottoman Empire. The action centers around a Moorish general, Othello, and his relationships with his wife Desdemona and his ensign Iago.

Key Aspects of Othello

Tone

Othello's tone is one of high tragedy, to match the serious and emotional themes explored in the play.

Setting

The majority of the play takes place in Cyprus, although the first act occurs in Venice.

Point of View

As a play, *Othello* has no traditional point of view the way a novel might, because the audience sees all of the action and there is no narrator.

Character Development

Othello, a Moorish general in the Venetian army, marries Desdemona, a Venetian noblewoman. The two have defied Desdemona's father and eloped, and hope to build a life together. Over the course of the play, Othello violently turns against Desdemona as a result of Iago's manipulations. Othello's jealous nature comes out and he commits horrible acts, killing his wife and then ending his own life out of guilt and grief.

Desdemona begins the play as a defiant and assertive woman, eloping with Othello and confident in her influence over him even in matters of state. At the play's end, however, she is meek and resigned to her fate and her loyalty to Othello, regardless of his violent intentions toward her.

Iago, the play's villain, remains a manipulative, dishonest, and cruel force throughout. He reveals these qualities as the play starts and only becomes more brutal as it goes on.

Themes

Appearance vs. Reality

This theme is especially relevant to Iago's character: although he is called "honest" and loyal by almost everyone in the play, he is treacherous, deceitful, and manipulative. As Othello begins to see the world through Iago's eyes, the distance between appearance and reality grows increasingly vast for him.

Race

Othello is a Moor in the midst of Venetian society, and he experiences significant prejudice from those around him. Race is also a factor when Othello perceives himself as a rough outsider, despite the fact that he is a well-respected general in the army. Othello's race still sets him apart, though, and it makes him self-conscious about his reputation, including its racial elements.

Pride

Othello is defensive of his reputation and his achievements, particularly because he feels he must overcompensate for his outsider status. The allegations of Desdemona's affair hurt his pride even more than they evoke his jealousy; their relationship is a very public one, and it helps him to appear powerful, accomplished, and morally upright.

Magic

Othello is charged with using magic to win over Desdemona, largely because he is black and therefore assumed to be pagan. Othello himself invokes magic when he tells Desdemona the story of her handkerchief's origins. Whether or not he believes his own story, Othello clearly believes in the symbolism and charm of the handkerchief, which is why the object is so significant to him.

Order vs. Chaos

As Iago exerts his influence over the characters of the play, chaos takes over. Othello's world in particular begins to be ruled by chaotic emotions and false allegations, as he begins to abandon reason.

Symbols

The Storm

The storm is a source of anxiety for the Venetians at Cyprus, who fear for the safety of Othello's ship. It also foreshadows the coming chaos: although Othello safely weathers the literal storm, he does not make it through the chaos that the storm represents.

Dark vs. Light

Darkness and blackness associated with immorality, disloyalty, and evil, while light and whiteness represent purity, innocence, and goodness. These symbols are particularly significant in Desdemona and Othello's relationship because of their respective races.

Desdemona's Handkerchief

The handkerchief is of great value to both Desdemona and Othello as a symbol of their relationship, in particular Desdemona's loyalty to Othello. Iago takes advantage of the handkerchief's symbolic importance and makes it central to his schemes.

Animals

Othello is frequently compared to animals, particularly when the characters discuss his sexual relationship with Desdemona. The imagery is demeaning and racially charged.

Climax

In Act III, Scene 3, Othello resolves with Iago to exact revenge on Cassio and Desdemona.

Structure

The play is divided into five acts, with the climax occurring in Act III.

Teaching Guide - Relationship with Other Books

Consider other plays or novels where betrayal and deception are central themes: Sophocles' Oedipus Cycle; Harold Pinter's *Betrayal*; Shakespeare's *Macbeth* or *Hamlet*.

Consider other works that focus on an unhappy or difficult marriage, such as Ibsen's *Hedda Gabler*; Tolstoy's *Anna Karenina*.

Teaching Guide - Bringing In Technology

The Reading Response Blog project, which should extend throughout the unit, requires internet-enabled devices for the students to write and post blog entries and comment on one another's blogs.

On Day 4, the Race, Gender and Culture activity requires internet-enabled devices, audio equipment, and could benefit from a way to play online video or DVDs. The Willow Song activity will also benefit from a way to play, and perhaps record, audio material.

On Day 5, screening film adaptations of *Othello* will require a way to play online video or DVDs.

Students might also utilize PowerPoint, dictation software, video recording and editing equipment, and other technologies throughout the unit.

Teaching Guide - Notes to the Teacher

Every classroom is different, but the key to teaching a play, whether it is in a literature course or a drama or theater course, is to bring the play alive in your classroom. Reading a play is a different experience from reading a novel; likewise, a play should be taught differently. This lesson plan includes activities and questions that can be used to encourage students to perform and see the play as a performative text, a text meant for actors, design, and stage interaction rather than reading alone.

The thought questions in this lesson plan provide material and ideas that students can use to write short original essays and to develop their powers of thought. For the sake of improving the power of expression, teachers should encourage students to write on topics that have been discussed in class, this time in the more formal writing style expected in a literary essay. At the same time, students should not be discouraged from choosing their own topics.

The questions provided for the final paper are most suitable for student essays. Remember that grading an essay should not depend on a simple checklist of required content.

Author of Lesson Plan and Sources

Michelle Rosenberg, author of Lesson Plan. Completed on January 22, 2014, copyright held by GradeSaver.

Updated and revised Gemma Cooper-Novack February 18, 2014. Copyright held by GradeSaver.

Shakespeare, William (ed. E. A. J. Honigmann). Othello. London: A & C Black Publishers Ltd., 1997.

Kochman, Susan M.. "MTV I[Othello]." 1998-11-01. 2014-01-15. <http://www.folger.edu/edulesplandtl.cfm?lpid=570>.

Harbaugh, Annmarie Kelly. ""How to choose a good Wife from bad?"." 2004-02-01. <http://www.folger.edu/eduLesPlanDtl.cfm?lpid=636>.

Related Links

http://www.folger.edu/documents/STC%2018514Discourse%20of%20marriage%20(3%20pag
"A Discourse on Marriage and Wiving" A 1615 pamphlet about marriage written by
Alexander Niccholes.

http://www.shakespearetheatre.org/plays/articles.aspx?&id=83
A Cultural Context for Othello A brief essay outlining the culture that informed the
play.

Day 1 - Reading Assignment

Read all of Act I.

Common Core Objectives

- CCSS.ELA-Literacy.CCRA.W.9
- CCSS.ELA-Literacy.CCRA.SL.1
- CCSS.ELA-Literacy.CCRA.L.4
- CCSS.ELA-Literacy.CCRA.SL.6

Note that it is perfectly fine to expand any day's work into two days depending on the characteristics of the class, particularly if the class will engage in all of the suggested classroom exercises and activities and discuss all of the thought questions.

Content Summary for Teachers

Act I, Scene i:

As the play opens, Roderigo and Iago (members of the Venetian army) are discussing the elopement of a general, Othello, with a noblewoman named Desdemona. Roderigo and Iago are both disgruntled; Roderigo has been in love with Desdemona for some time, and Iago is resentful because Othello has recently passed him over for a promotion.

The two men call upon Brabantio, Desdemona's father, to inform him of Desdemona's elopement with Othello in the hopes that he will be alarmed and angry. Brabantio is angry at being awoken by Roderigo, whom he has apparently forbidden from his home after Roderigo's repeated attempts to court Desdemona. Brabantio nonetheless wakes up his household to investigate the whereabouts of his daughter; when he finds that she is gone, Brabantio is furious. Roderigo offers to lead Brabantio to where he believes Desdemona and Othello to be.

Act I, Scene ii: Iago informs Othello that Roderigo has conveyed the news of his marriage to Desdemona's father. Cassio arrives and announces that the duke has summoned Othello to Cyprus on an important matter. Iago threatens Roderigo with violence, making a false show of his loyalty to Othello. Brabantio arrives with Roderigo and threatens Othello, accusing him of enchanting Desdemona with dark magic. Brabantio is certain that the duke and other legal authorities will side with him in the case.

Act I, Scene iii:

Reports indicate that the Turkish fleet is advancing toward Cyprus, which has until now been a Venetian stronghold. Brabantio arrives and tells the assembled senators about his grievance against Othello. Othello defends himself and Desdemona affirms that their courtship was mutual. The council finds in favor of Othello, determining that the couple will stay married.

The Duke sends Othello to Cyprus to command the Venetian army there. Othello agrees to the post and assigns Iago to take care of Desdemona, who will be joining them in Cyprus. After Othello and Desdemona leave, Roderigo continues to despair about losing Desdemona, threatening to kill himself over it. Iago advises him to save up his money and wait until Othello and Desdemona have a falling out, which he assures Roderigo will not take long. Iago also pledges to help Roderigo and reaffirms his hatred for Othello; it is becoming clear that Iago plans to break up Othello's marriage and is merely using Roderigo as a means to that end.

Thought Questions (students consider while they read)

1. Why is it ironic that Iago is often called "honest" and "true," particularly by Othello?
2. Think about the language that other characters have used to talk about Othello so far. How does it serve to degrade, dehumanize, and generally "other" him?
3. According to Othello, what made Desdemona fall in love with him?
4. What does Iago believe about reason vs. emotion and our ability to mediate between those forces? (See I.iii.318-362 for his conversation with Roderigo about these ideas.) Do you agree or disagree?
5. What do you think is Iago's true motivation, based on his words and actions so far?

Vocabulary (in order of appearance)

I.i.23:

- Spinster: An unmarried older woman

I.i.47:

- Provender: Food or provisions, usually for animals

I.i.68:

- Incense: To make angry

I.i.71:

- Vexation: Frustration or annoyance

I.i.85:

- Zounds: An exclamation (derived from the phrase "By God's wounds!")

I.i.99:

- Malicious: Having bad intentions

I.i.124:

- Lascivious: Overtly sexual; lewd

I.i.160:

- Nought: Nothing

I.ii.27:

- Circumscription: A delineated space or area

I.iii.24:

- Facile: Easy or effortless

I.iii.41:

- Valiant: Courageous and determined

I.iii.67:

- Beguiled: Enchanted or deceived

I.iii.72:

- Mandate: An order or decree

I.iii.329:

- Baseness: A lack of morals

Additional Homework

1. Do some brief research on one of the following: the original story that inspired Shakespeare's *Othello* ("A Moorish Captain," by Cinthio); or the Ottoman-Venetian War (1570-73), which provides the play's setting. Write a paragraph about what you learn.

Day 1 - Discussion of Thought Questions

1. Why is it ironic that Iago is often called "honest" and "true," particularly by Othello?

   Time: 5 min

   Discussion: Iago is clearly plotting against Othello, although it is not clear where his loyalties actually lie or why he wants to harm Othello. Iago is deceptive and cruel, but Othello trusts him deeply. The trust that both Othello and Roderigo put in Iago is gravely misplaced; constant references to Iago's apparent honesty and loyalty serve to underscore this fact.

2. Think about the language that other characters have used to talk about Othello so far. How does it serve to degrade, dehumanize, and generally "other" him?

   Time: 7-10 min

   Discussion: Brabantio, Iago, and Roderigo consistently compare Othello to animals (horses, rams, etc.), especially when making lewd comments about Othello and Desdemona's marital life. They also make derogatory comments about his race—to them, his blackness allies him with immorality, dark magic, and excessive lust. Even the Duke, who has great respect for Othello, compliments him by saying Othello is whiter in his morals than in his complexion.

3. According to Othello, what made Desdemona fall in love with him?

   Time: 5-7 min

   Discussion: Othello argues that it was his stories of heroism and adventure that intrigued Desdemona. He demonstrates a flair for language as he makes his case to the council, and he seems to believe that his talents for storytelling have won over Desdemona's affections.

4. What does Iago believe about reason vs. emotion and our ability to mediate between those forces? (See I.iii.318-362 for his conversation with Roderigo about these ideas.) Do you agree or disagree?

Time: 7-10 min

Discussion: Iago tells Roderigo to stop giving in to his emotions, which Iago believes reflects weakness. Rather than killing himself or simply despairing, Iago thinks that Roderigo should channel his anger and depression into practical pursuits, like putting away money for the inevitable time when Desdemona leaves Othello. Students should evaluate Iago's perspective based on their own experiences and other works of art that they have encountered.

5. What do you think is Iago's true motivation, based on his words and actions so far?

Time: 7-10 min

Discussion: Iago has lied to both Roderigo and Othello about his loyalties. His professed motivation is his own gain, although aside from advancing his military career it is not entirely clear yet how Iago intends to benefit from his schemes. It's possible that Iago's motivation is indeed simple self-gain, as he has stated so far. However, given his propensity for lying, it might be worth questioning his claims about his own motivations. (Iago is also frequently held up as an example of a purely evil character, an archetypical villain, but this might be a less fruitful course of discussion.)

Day 1 - Short Answer Quiz

1. Roderigo is in love with _____.

_____

2. How does Brabantio react to the news of his daughter's elopement?

_____

3. What is Iago's relationship to Othello?

_____

4. How does Othello describe Iago?

_____

5. What makes Othello different from the Venetians around him?

_____

6. Of what does Brabantio accuse Othello?

_____

7. What convinces the military council to find in Othello's favor?

_____

8. Why does Othello want for Desdemona while he is away in Cyprus?

_____

9. What does Roderigo threaten to do when he finds out that Desdemona has married Othello?

_____

10. What does Iago tell Roderigo to do regarding Desdemona?

_____

Short Answer Quiz Key

1. Desdemona.
2. Answers should note that Brabantio is alarmed and angry, and might reference the fact that Brabantio attempts to have a military council punish Othello for marrying Desdemona.
3. Iago is Othello's ensign in the Venetian army, meaning that he reports directly to Othello.
4. Othello calls him honest, loyal, and true.
5. Othello is of a different race (students might write specifically that Othello is black, or "Moorish").
6. Brabantio argues that Othello has effectively stolen his daughter by bewitching her with dark magic.
7. Answers should mention either Othello's eloquent and moving testimony, Desdemona's clear statement that she was not tricked, or a combination of the two.
8. Othello wants Desdemona to have a home that befits her status, including an appropriate level of comfort, stimulating activities and entertainment, and people to engage with.
9. He threatens to kill himself.
10. Iago tells Roderigo to save up his money and bide his time until Desdemona and Othello have a falling out.

Day 1 - Crossword Puzzle

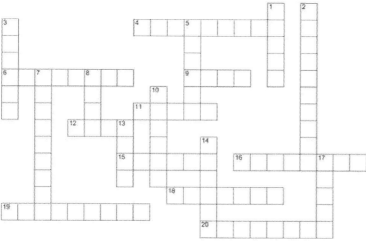

ACROSS

4. Food or provisions.
6. _____ threatens to kill himself over Desdemona.
9. The play's villain.
11. Iago tells Roderigo to save his _____.
12. Othello is a _____.
15. Othello promotes _____ to lieutenant.
16. An older, unmarried woman.
18. Othello's military rank.
19. Desdemona's father.
20. The council of _____ finds in Othello's favor.

DOWN

1. Iago advises Rodergo to _____ puppies.
2. Lewd
3. The army sends Othello to _____.
5. Where the first act takes place.
7. Othello's wife.
8. Othello's ensign.
10. Othello often describes Iago as _____.
13. Othello's _____ makes him different.
14. An exclamation.
17. The Venetians are at war with the _____.

Crossword Puzzle Answer Key

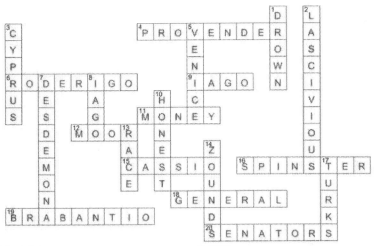

ACROSS

4. Food or provisions.
6. _____ threatens to kill himself over Desdemona.
9. The play's villain.
11. Iago tells Roderigo to save his _____.
12. Othello is a _____.
15. Othello promotes _____ to lieutenant.
16. An older, unmarried woman.
18. Othello's military rank.
19. Desdemona's father.
20. The council of _____ finds in Othello's favor.

DOWN

1. Iago advises Rodergo to _____ puppies.
2. Lewd
3. The army sends Othello to _____.
5. Where the first act takes place.
7. Othello's wife.
8. Othello's ensign.
10. Othello often describes Iago as _____.
13. Othello's _____ makes him different.
14. An exclamation.
17. The Venetians are at war with the _____.

Day 1 - Vocabulary Quiz

Terms	Answers
1. ____ Incense	A. Lack of morals
2. ____ Zounds	B. A delineated space or area
3. ____ Malicious	C. Ill-intentioned
4. ____ Facile	D. Easy, effortless
5. ____ Circumscription	E. An exclamation (derived from the phrase
6. ____ Mandate	"By God's wounds!")
7. ____ Nought	F. Annoyance
8. ____ Baseness	G. Nothing
9. ____ Valiant	H. An order or decree
10. ____ Vexation	I. To make angry
	J. Courageous and determined

Vocabulary Quiz Answer Key

1. I
2. E
3. C
4. D
5. B
6. H
7. G
8. A
9. J
10. F

Day 1 - Classroom Activities

1. *Othello* in Context

   Kind of Activity: Group Discussion
   Objective: To provide the historical background necessary to grasp the relationships and action of the play.
   Common Core State Standards: CCSS.ELA-Literacy.CCRA.W.9 ; CCSS.ELA-Literacy.CCRA.SL.1
   Time: 25 min

   Structure:

   Ask the students what they know about either Shakespeare's time, or the time in which the play is set (they might have gleaned this knowledge from previous courses, from the book's notes, etc.). Write down some general impressions that come up, and then break the students into groups. Provide specific questions and have students break into groups to answer them. This might involve Internet research, handouts with historical information, or the introduction to their edition of the play. Give each group a different set of 5-6 questions to answer, and then re-convene the entire class to share everyone's findings. The result should provide a good overview of the historical context and social mores at work in *Othello*.

   Discussion Questions:

   • Who were the Moors?

   • Who were the Venetians?

   • With whom were the Venetians at war and why?

   • What was the role of women?

   • What rules for getting married existed at the time of the play?

   Ideans for Differentiated Instruction:

   -Provide research sources for a variety of skill levels, and ensure that students have access to appropriate sources for their needs.

   -Provide visual tools (graphic organizers, diagrams, word maps, etc.) to help students organize their notes and develop answers to the research questions.

Assessment Ideas:

-Have students turn in their notes to the instructor for evaluation.

-Evaluate students' contributions to both the classwide and group discussions.

2. Performing *Othello*

Kind of Activity: Performance
Objective: To allow students to experience the play in a dramatic, rather than literary, context.
Common Core State Standards: CCSS.ELA-Literacy.CCRA.L.4 ;
CCSS.ELA-Literacy.CCRA.SL.6
Time: 40 min

Structure:

Choose several excerpts from the first act and break the students into groups. Assign each group an excerpt and allow them to practice briefly before performing their section for the class as a whole. Remind them to pay specific attention to unfamiliar words and phrases, and to decipher them so that they can perform the scene with a better understanding.

After the performances, have each group begin working together to translate the text of their assigned excerpt into modern English. On Day 2, the groups will continue this work and then present the modern-English version of their scene to the class, discuss the process, and explore Shakespearian language further.

Ideans for Differentiated Instruction:

-Provide resources for looking up unfamiliar words and references, and circulate among the groups to offer help.

-Assign roles based on students' individual levels of fluency and comfort reading aloud and performing in front of others.

Assessment Ideas:

-Evaluate the students' performances in terms of their reading fluency, demonstrated comprehension, and ability to convey meaning and nuance.

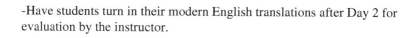

-Have students turn in their modern English translations after Day 2 for evaluation by the instructor.

Day 2 - Reading Assignment

Read all of Act II.

Common Core Objectives

- CCSS.ELA-Literacy.CCRA.W.4
- CCSS.ELA-Literacy.CCRA.R.3
- CCSS.ELA-Literacy.CCRA.L.4
- CCSS.ELA-Literacy.CCRA.SL.6

Note that it is perfectly fine to expand any day's work into two days depending on the characteristics of the class, particularly if the class will engage in all of the suggested classroom exercises and activities and discuss all of the thought questions.

Content Summary for Teachers

Act II, Scene i: A storm hits Cyprus, possibly staving off the Turkish invasion. A messenger announces that Cassio has arrived, but Othello's ship is still at sea. Iago and Desdemona arrive (along with Roderigo and Emilia), which is surprising because their ship left a week after those of Cassio and Othello. Iago expounds on his views about women, namely that they are unworthy of praise and talk too much; Desdemona argues with him. Iago notes, to the audience, that he sees an opportunity to turn Othello against Cassio by planting the idea that he and Desdemona are having an affair. Othello arrives safely and announces that the Turks are no longer a danger, having been wiped out by the storm. Left alone with Roderigo, Iago convinces him that Desdemona is in love with Cassio; Roderigo agrees to attack Cassio that evening. Left alone, Iago tells us that he believes his wife Emilia has had an affair with Othello, and Iago is seeking revenge.

Act II, Scene ii: Othello's herald announces that everyone is invited to a celebration that will commemorate both Othello and Desdemona's marriage and the defeat of the Turks.

Act II, Scene iii:

Iago and Cassio are on night watch duty. Iago attempts to get Cassio drunk in the hope of starting a fight between him and Roderigo. Iago also tries to convince Cassio that Desdemona has been flirting with him—Iago is trying on several fronts to discredit Cassio so that his position as lieutenant will be in jeopardy.

Other soldiers, including Montano, join Iago and Cassio in drinking, singing and chatting. When Cassio leaves briefly, Iago tells Montano that Cassio has a drinking problem, which might impede his abilities as lieutenant. When Roderigo arrives, Iago tells him to go after Cassio. A fight ensues involving Cassio, Roderigo, and

Montano. When Othello arrives, Iago claims that Cassio started the fight in a fit of drunkenness. Othello strips Cassio of his position, and Cassio laments the ruin of his reputation. Iago tells Cassio not to be so hard on himself, and advises him that the best way to return to Othello's good graces is by winning over Desdemona.

Thought Questions (students consider while they read)

1. Consider Iago's stated reasons for manipulating and deceiving people. Are the reasons that he reveals in Act II convincing?
2. How does Cassio treat and speak about women in this act? Compare this to the ideas that Iago expresses about women.
3. What method(s) does Iago use to make his lies more believable?
4. Why is the storm significant?
5. What do you make of the extended discussion of England among the soldiers, given that the play takes place in Cyprus among an army of Venetians?

Vocabulary (in order of appearance)

II.i.21:

- Tempest: storm

II.i.50:

- Surfeited: overly full or satiated

II.i.62:

- Paragon: a model or prime example of a particular quality

II.i.92:

- Citadel: Fortress

II.i.114:

- Slanderer: One who tells malicious lies meant to hurt another person's reputation

II.i.126:

- Pate: Head

II.i.165:

- Relish: Appreciate or savor

II.i.196:

- Discord: Strife or disagreement

II.i.222:

- Prating: Talking inanely and at length

II.i.245:

- Pestilent: Deadly

II.i.307:

- Egregiously: Excessively

II.iii.16:

- Wanton: Sexually charged

II.iii.22:

- Provocation: A challenge

II.iii.38:

- Infirmity: Weakness or sickliness

II.iii.73:

- Potent: Powerful

II.iii.227:

- Clamour: Loud noise

II.iii.260:

- Bestial: Animalistic

II.iii.271:

- Imperious: Overbearing, arrogant

II.iii.318:

- Entreat: To plead with

II.iii.340:

- Enfettered: Containing obstacles

II.iii.368:

- Dilatory: Slow-acting

Additional Homework

1. Write an additional entry in your Reading Response Blog. This entry can cover anything from Act I or II and should be at least one page long. Be prepared to share it with a partner in class.

Day 2 - Discussion of Thought Questions

1. Consider Iago's stated reasons for manipulating and deceiving people. Are the reasons that he reveals in Act II convincing?

   Time: 7-10 min

   Discussion: Iago claims to be acting on his own self-interest in two ways: 1) getting Cassio fired so that Iago can take over his position as lieutenant; and 2) getting revenge on Othello because Iago believes that Othello and Emilia have had an affair. These might be convincing reasons for Iago's actions, but as his manipulations become more and more elaborate and begin to ruin lives, it might seem to some readers that Iago has merely concocted excuses for his cruel impulses.

2. How does Cassio treat and speak about women in this act? Compare this to the ideas that Iago expresses about women.

   Time: 5-7 min

   Discussion: Cassio is respectful and even reverent of women, speaking particularly well of Desdemona. Iago, on the other hand, rants about how manipulative and deceitful women are (ironic since Iago himself is defined by those qualities), and complains that they speak their mind far too often. He also makes lewd sexual comments about Desdemona and about his own wife Emilia.

3. What method(s) does Iago use to make his lies more believable?

   Time: 5-7 min

   Discussion: Iago anticipates what his audience wants to hear, and acts as though he is on their side. For instance, he pretends to be upset and disbelieving when he lies to Othello about Cassio starting the fight among the soldiers. Iago convinces people that he is acting in their best interests, when in fact he is manipulating them.

4. Why is the storm significant?

Time: 5-7 min

Discussion: On a practical level, the storm delays Othello's arrival at Cyprus and also prevents the Turkish invasion of the island. But the storm can also be seen as foreshadowing the chaos to come, as Iago continues to deceive everyone and cause chaos in their lives and in the Venetian military.

5. What do you make of the extended discussion of England among the soldiers, given that the play takes place in Cyprus among an army of Venetians?

Time: 5 min

Discussion: The soldiers talk of England with great respect, noting what formidable drinkers the English are. Iago even sings a song about the country. This praise for England was likely a way for Shakespeare to please the audience and get a reaction from the crowd during productions of the play.

Day 2 - Short Answer Quiz

1. Iago instigates a fight between whom during the night watch?

_____

2. What happens to the advancing Turkish fleet?

_____

3. What do Iago and Desdemona argue about?

_____

4. How does Othello react when he hears that Cassio has started a fight?

_____

5. How does Cassio plan to get his position back?

_____

6. Who is Iago's wife?

_____

7. What are the soldiers celebrating?

_____

8. What does Iago say is Cassio's great weakness?

_____

9. What idea does Iago intend to plant in Othello's mind about Desdemona?

_____

10. What personal offense does Iago suspect Othello has committed against him?

_____

Short Answer Quiz Key

1. Cassio and Roderigo.
2. Its ships are wrecked in the storm.
3. They argue about the nature of women.
4. He fires Cassio from his position as lieutenant.
5. He plans to get Desdemona on his side first, as Iago has advised him to do.
6. Emilia.
7. They are celebrating both Othello and Desdemona's marriage and the announcement that the Turks will not be attacking.
8. He cannot control himself around alcohol.
9. He wants Othello to believe that Desdemona and Cassio are having an affair.
10. He believes that Othello has had an affair with Emilia.

Day 2 - Crossword Puzzle

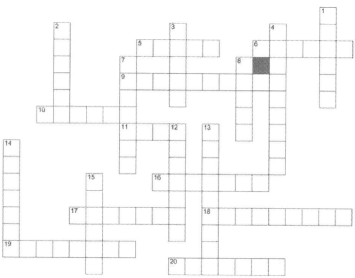

ACROSS

5. The ____ wipes out the Turkish fleet.
6. Appreciate or savor.
9. Containing obstacles.
10. Powerful.
11. He starts the fight during night watch
16. Iago wants _____ on Othello.
17. Fortress
18. Weakness
19. He plans to attack Cassio.
20. Strife

DOWN

1. Who is on night watch duty with Iago?
2. _____ does not actually love Desdemona.
3. Iago expresses disdain for all _____.
4. Othello starts to believe Iago about _____.
7. Animalistic
8. The soldiers get ____ during their watch.
12. _____ strips Cassio of his rank.
13. Overbearing
14. Loud noise
15. Iago's wife.

Crossword Puzzle Answer Key

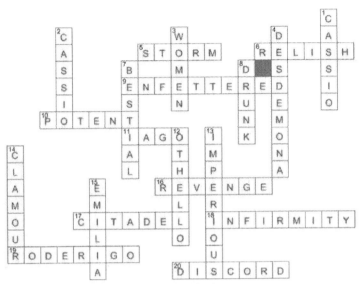

ACROSS

5. The ____ wipes out the Turkish fleet.
6. Appreciate or savor.
9. Containing obstacles.
10. Powerful.
11. He starts the fight during night watch
16. Iago wants _____ on Othello.
17. Fortress
18. Weakness
19. He plans to attack Cassio.
20. Strife

DOWN

1. Who is on night watch duty with Iago?
2. _____ does not actually love Desdemona.
3. Iago expresses disdain for all _____.
4. Othello starts to believe Iago about _____.
7. Animalistic
8. The soldiers get ____ during their watch.
12. _____ strips Cassio of his rank.
13. Overbearing
14. Loud noise
15. Iago's wife.

Day 2 - Vocabulary Quiz

Terms

1. ____ Tempest
2. ____ Pate
3. ____ Prating
4. ____ Wanton
5. ____ Bestial
6. ____ Clamour
7. ____ Paragon
8. ____ Infirmity
9. ____ Discord
10. ____ Slanderer

Answers

A. Strife

B. Weakness

C. A loud noise

D. A model or prime example

E. One who tells malicious lies meant to hurt another person's reputation

F. Animalistic

G. Storm

H. Sexually charged

I. Head

J. Talking inanely and at length

Vocabulary Quiz Answer Key

1. G
2. I
3. J
4. H
5. F
6. C
7. D
8. B
9. A
10. E

Day 2 - Classroom Activities

1. "Translating" Shakespeare

Kind of Activity: Performance
Objective: To help students understand Shakespearian language and vocabulary.
Common Core State Standards: CCSS.ELA-Literacy.CCRA.L.4 ; CCSS.ELA-Literacy.CCRA.SL.6
Time: 40 min

Structure:

Have students break into their groups from Part I and give them time to finish their modern-language "translations." Once again, be sure to provide appropriate reference texts and roam around the classroom to help any students who are struggling.

When they've finished writing, have each group perform their brief scene. The students who are not performing should follow along with the scene in their own texts to compare the original with their peers' interpretations. After each group has performed, facilitate a discussion. Some questions to cover might include:

-What was most challenging about translating the text into modern English? (Particular words? Idiomatic expressions? Cultural references?)

-How did your experience of performing the text change after doing the translation work?

-Did the exercise improve your understanding of the scene?

After the discussion, ask what words or phrases were new to them in Act II. How did they approach these unfamiliar words (did they use context clues, read footnotes, look them up separately, etc.)? Make a list of words, phrases, or references that are still puzzling students and work through them together. You may also want to discuss Shakespeare's role in originating certain words, including many that the students might come across every day.

Ideans for Differentiated Instruction: -Provide multiple types of reference resources for different learning styles: texts, websites, audio pronunciation guides, etc.

Assessment Ideas:

-Evaluate the students' performances in terms of their reading fluency, demonstrated comprehension, and ability to convey meaning and nuance.

-Have students turn in their modern English translations for evaluation.

2. Reading Response Blogs

Kind of Activity: Individual Writing
Objective: To allow students to respond individually to the events, characters, and language of the play.
Common Core State Standards: CCSS.ELA-Literacy.CCRA.W.6; CCSS.ELA-Literacy.CCRA.W.10 ; CCSS.ELA-Literacy.CCRA.R.3
Time: 30 min

Structure:

Have students set up individual blogs using a free, simple blogging website. These blogs will serve as a place to respond to the play throughout the unit. After setting up, give the class a few minutes to write independently about their responses to Act II of the play in a blog post. They might pick a particular scene to respond to, or explore a character's development so far, or they might prefer to discuss the language and poetry of the play. Encourage them to delve into whatever aspects of the play they find most interesting.

After the students have written their first blog entry, ask them to pair up and exchange URLs with a partner. The students should read one another's work and discuss their ideas together. Encourage them to ask why their partner chose a particular scene/character/monologue, and to explore where their opinions and feelings about the play might differ. Remind them to support their opinions with evidence from the text.

Ask students to continue writing blog entries—at least two per act, and more if they are so inclined—for the duration of the unit. On subsequent days they will continue to share their responses with a partner and generate discussions together. Another option is to share the blog URLs with the entire class and allow anyone to comment at any time, perhaps requiring a certain number of responses per student per week.

Ideans for Differentiated Instruction:

-Suggest topics or provide prompts for students who are unsure of where to begin.

-Provide visual tools, such as character maps, flow charts, or other organizers for students to use to begin their writing process.

-Consider allowing students to record audio or video entries instead of written ones.

Assessment Ideas:
-Evaluate the blog entries and comments as they are updated. Also consider commenting on the students' blogs directly as part of the ongoing dialogue.

Day 3 - Reading Assignment

Read all of Act III.

Common Core Objectives

- CCSS.ELA-Literacy.CCRA.R.5
- CCSS.ELA-Literacy.CCRA.L.5
- CCSS.ELA-Literacy.CCRA.W.6
- CCSS.ELA-Literacy.CCRA.W.10
- CCSS.ELA-Literacy.CCRA.R.3

Note that it is perfectly fine to expand any day's work into two days depending on the characteristics of the class, particularly if the class will engage in all of the suggested classroom exercises and activities and discuss all of the thought questions.

Content Summary for Teachers

Act III, Scene i: A group of musicians and a clown provide some comic relief, and then Cassio asks the clown to see if Desdemona will speak with him. Iago's wife Emilia relates to Cassio some of the conversations that have transpired about him between Desdemona and Othello: Desdemona has spoken well of Cassio so far. Emilia offers to advocate for Cassio with Desdemona.

Act III, Scene ii: Othello and Iago prepare to walk the grounds of the fortress. Othello gives Iago some letters to be sent to Venice.

Act III, Scene iii:

Desdemona, Cassio, and Emilia discuss Cassio's predicament. Desdemona promises to do all she can on Cassio's behalf. Cassio leaves as Othello and Iago come in, and Iago takes the opportunity to point out Cassio's quick departure as suspicious. Desdemona then tells Othello that she is concerned about Cassio and wants them to reconcile; she begs Othello to invite Cassio to dine with them in the next few days so that they can work things out. When Desdemona leaves with Emilia, Iago attempts to make Othello paranoid about Cassio, implying that he cannot be trusted with Desdemona and that the two might be having an affair. Othello becomes convinced that this is a real possibility and that he must be on the lookout for evidence.

Desdemona and Emilia return, and Desdemona accidentally drops her handkerchief before she and Othello leave for dinner. Emilia picks it up, noting that it was a present from Othello and of great sentimental value for both him and Desdemona. Iago has long wanted Emilia to steal the handkerchief, so she takes it in order to please him. Iago enters and is happy to receive the stolen handkerchief, telling the audience that he plans to plant it in Cassio's lodgings to elicit further suspicion from

Othello.

Othello re-enters. He is being driven mad imagining Desdemona's unfaithfulness and demands that Iago show him proof of the affair. Iago says that he has heard Cassio talk in his sleep about Desdemona, and that he has seen Cassio using her handkerchief. Othello is then convinced, and vows to have Cassio killed and take revenge on Desdemona.

Act III, Scene iv:

Desdemona asks the clown to find Cassio for her. She is deeply upset at losing her handkerchief and looks for it everywhere; she knows that Othello will be unhappy if it's lost. When Othello enters, he asks Desdemona for her handkerchief, which she admits she doesn't have. Othello says the handkerchief has magical powers and implies that she will suffer for losing it or giving it away. Othello becomes obsessed with the handkerchief and demands that Desdemona show it to him, but instead she persists in trying to get Othello to meet with Cassio. Othello storms off.

Cassio and Othello enter, and Cassio laments that he cannot seem to reconcile with Othello. Desdemona sympathizes and says she is worried about Othello's recent odd behavior. Iago leaves, pretending to go and check on Othello. Emilia thinks that Othello's behavior is due to jealousy, but Desdemona insists it must be matters of state that are distracting and upsetting him. Bianca, Cassio's mistress, arrives. Cassio gives her Desdemona's handkerchief as a gift, mentioning that he found it in his quarters.

Thought Questions (students consider while they read)

1. Consider Desdemona's relationship with Othello. What is the power dynamic?
2. How are Othello and Iago different in their judgments of other people?
3. How does Iago speak? Is his speech different from those of other characters? What effect does his speech have on others?
4. How does Iago undermine Othello's confidence in Desdemona?
5. What is the role of the clown? Does he have any significance beyond comic relief?

Vocabulary (in order of appearance)

III.i.47:

- Affinity: Attraction

III.iii.24:

Content Summary for Teachers

- Shrift: Confession (as with a priest)

III.iii.43:

- Languish: To become weak

III.iii.90:

- Perdition: Destruction, especially in a religious sense

III.iii.118:

- Conceit: Idea or concept

III.iii.169:

- Cuckold: A man whose wife is cheating on him

III.iii.255:

- Vehement: Passionate or forceful

III.iii.354:

- Steed: Horse

III.iii.359:

- Counterfeit: To imitate or falsify

III.iii.463:

- Reverence: Deep respect

III.iv.41:

- Castigation: Punishment

III.iv.75:

- Hallowed: Made holy; consecrated

III.iv.123:

- Alms: Charity

Additional Homework

1. Create a character map that you think captures the relationships at play so far. Include, at minimum, Othello, Desdemona, Iago, Roderigo, and Cassio.

Day 3 - Discussion of Thought Questions

1. Consider Desdemona's relationship with Othello. What is the power dynamic?

   Time: 5-7 min

   Discussion: Desdemona seems to think that she has quite a bit of influence over Othello, as she tells Cassio that she'll have no problem getting him back into Othello's good graces. But as the story progresses and Iago poisons Othello against Desdemona, it becomes clear that the real power in the marriage lies with Othello.

2. How are Othello and Iago different in their judgments of other people?

   Time: 7-10 min

   Discussion: Othello always wants to see people's virtues; he recognizes Cassio's talents and perhaps misses his weakness around alcohol. Iago, on the other hand, is always looking for weaknesses to exploit. Iago even admits this, telling Othello directly that he tends to see the worst in people and perhaps create flaws where none are really present. Of course, Iago says this largely in order to gain Othello's trust so that he will be more prone to believe Iago's lies about Cassio.

3. How does Iago speak? Is his speech different from those of other characters? What effect does his speech have on others?

   Time: 7-10 min

   Discussion: Iago almost speaks in riddles; his speeches are often iterative, if not outright repetitive. He makes strange generalizations that sound vaguely like cliches, but their meanings are often obscure. The effect is to drive those around him mad as they try to determine his true meaning. Of course, he is doing this quite deliberately and skillfully, so even when people are able to unravel Iago's metaphors and platitudes, they are still not learning the truth.

4. How does Iago undermine Othello's confidence in Desdemona?

Time: 5-7 min

Discussion: Iago argues that Desdemona has already revealed herself capable of deception: she lied to her father about her relationship with Othello, to the point that Brabantio knew nothing of their love until they eloped. Iago also impugns Venetian women in general, claiming that they are by nature duplicitous.

5. What is the role of the clown? Does he have any significance beyond comic relief?

Time: 5-7 min

Discussion: The clown (like the musicians, in their brief appearance) is primarily a source of comic relief. However, much of his humor comes from puns, quasi-riddles, and other ways of speaking that confuse those around him. In this way he is quite similar to Iago.

Day 3 - Short Answer Quiz

1. Who is Bianca?

_____

2. Why does Iago want Desdemona's handkerchief?

_____

3. What is Emilia's explanation for Othello's strange behavior?

_____

4. How does Desdemona explain Othello's behavior?

_____

5. What two pieces of evidence does Iago give Othello for Desdemona's affair?

_____

6. How does Othello intend to get revenge on Cassio?

_____

7. Why does Desdemona want Othello to invite Cassio to dine with them?

_____

8. Why is the handkerchief important to Desdemona?

_____

9. Why is Bianca suspicious when Cassio gives her the handkerchief?

_____

10. How does Othello's view of Desdemona change during this act?

_____

Short Answer Quiz Key

1. Cassio's mistress.
2. He plans to plant it in Cassio's quarters as "proof" of their affair.
3. She believes that he is jealous, or paranoid about Desdemona's behavior in some way.
4. She thinks he is preoccupied with a government matter that is upsetting him deeply.
5. He claims to have heard Cassio talk about Desdemona in his sleep, and he claims that he saw Desdemona's handkerchief in Cassio's rooms.
6. He intends to have Cassio killed.
7. She wants to convince Othello to reconcile with Cassio.
8. Othello gave it to her early in their courtship.
9. She is worried that Cassio has been unfaithful to her and the handkerchief belongs to some other lover.
10. He starts out believing that Desdemona is pure and virtuous and unable to do any wrong. Iago slowly convinces Othello over the course of the act that Desdemona is an adulterer and a liar.

Day 3 - Crossword Puzzle

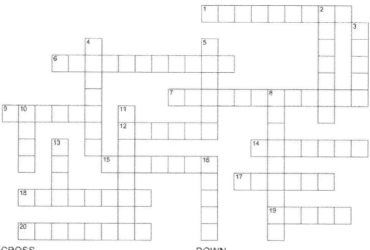

ACROSS
1. Deep respect
6. To imitate or falsify
7. What does Desdemona drop?
9. Desdemona advocates for _____.
12. _____ offers to talk to Desdemona for Cassio.
14. Othello vows to get _____ on Desdemona.
15. Iago is to send _____ to Venice.
17. Emilia _____ the handkerchief from Desdemona handkerchief.
18. Made holy
19. Who provides comic relief?
20. Attraction

DOWN
2. Idea or concept
3. Othello wants to see _____ of the affair.
4. A man whose wife is unfaithful.
5. Cassio gives the handkerchief to _____.
8. Deep respect
10. Charity
11. Passionate
13. Othello swears to _____ Cassio.
16. Horse

Crossword Puzzle Answer Key

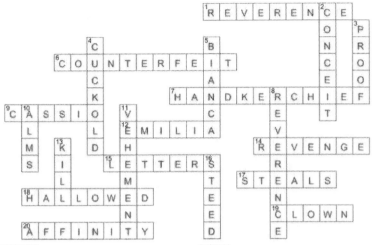

ACROSS

1. Deep respect
6. To imitate or falsify
7. What does Desdemona drop?
9. Desdemona advocates for _____.
12. _____ offers to talk to Desdemona for Cassio.
14. Othello vows to get _____ on Desdemona.
15. Iago is to send _____ to Venice.
17. Emilia _____ the handkerchief from Desdemona handkerchief.
18. Made holy
19. Who provides comic relief?
20. Attraction

DOWN

2. Idea or concept
3. Othello wants to see _____ of the affair.
4. A man whose wife is unfaithful.
5. Cassio gives the handkerchief to _____.
8. Deep respect
10. Charity
11. Passionate
13. Othello swears to _____ Cassio.
16. Horse

Day 3 - Vocabulary Quiz

Terms

1. ____ Shrift
2. ____ Perdition
3. ____ Cuckold
4. ____ Steed
5. ____ Reverence
6. ____ Alms
7. ____ Castigation
8. ____ Vehement

Answers

A. Confession (as with a priest)
B. Punishment
C. Passionate or forceful
D. A man whose wife is cheating on him
E. Horse
F. Destruction or damnation
G. Charity
H. Deep respect

Vocabulary Quiz Answer Key

1. A
2. F
3. D
4. E
5. H
6. G
7. B
8. C

Day 3 - Classroom Activities

1. Verse, Meter, and Character

   Kind of Activity: Classwide Discussion
   Objective: To understand how character development can be played out in verse and meter
   Common Core State Standards: CCSS.ELA-Literacy.CCRA.R.5 ; CCSS.ELA-Literacy.CCRA.L.5
   Time: 45 min

   Structure:

   Start by refreshing the students' memories about the concepts of meter and verse, focusing in particular on iambic pentameter. Then, pick part of a scene from Act III and ask for student volunteers to read it aloud. As those students read, the rest of the students should try to annotate their own texts (provide photocopies for this purpose) to note the meter and, perhaps, rhyme scheme. You might break the students into groups and assign each group a set of lines to take notes on. Once the scene has been read aloud, discuss as a class any lines that were difficult to scan, or lines that had no meter at all. Questions for discussion include:

   -Why might Shakespeare have broken meter in those lines?

   -Was the character particularly emotional? If so, how does the meter enhance that?

   -Was it a full break in the meter, or merely an extra or missing syllable?

   -When do two characters share lines of iambic pentameter (for instance, Emilia and Desdemona often do), and what might that indicate?

   -Are there any instances of prose in this scene? Who is speaking them?

   -Going back to previous scenes, has the meter associated with any particular character changed? Does it follow the arc of their character?

   Ideans for Differentiated Instruction:

   -Work through some examples as a class before asking students to scan the text directly.

   -Encourage the use of clapping or tapping pens to help determine meter, rather than just writing down symbols above each syllable.

Assessment Ideas:

-Have each student turn in their annotated text for evaluation.

-Assess students' contributions to the class discussion and their behavior while working in groups.

2. Reading Response Blogs

Kind of Activity: Group Work
Objective: To allow students to give each other feedback on their writing and discuss the play in small groups.
Common Core State Standards: CCSS.ELA-Literacy.CCRA.W.6
Time: 25 min

Structure:

Students should have written at least two entries in their Reading Response Blogs for Act III. Have them pair up and read one another's entries, comment on the blog, and then discuss whatever aspects they find most interesting. Encourage them to ask why their partner chose a particular scene/character/monologue, and to explore where their opinions and feelings about the play might differ. Remind them to support their opinions with evidence from the text. They might also want to explore whether any themes or motifs are emerging in their blogs so far, or whether any ideas for essays or final projects might have come up among their writings.

After working in pairs, have the class re-group and ask each pair of students to share one or two things that came up in their journal entries or discussion. Allow for extended discussion on any points that seem to be of interest to the class as a whole. This activity can be continued throughout the rest of the unit.

Ideans for Differentiated Instruction:

-Continue to allow students to record audio or video journal entries to post to their blogs if they wish.

-Pair students based on differing strengths and weaknesses, so that they can help each other improve.

Assessment Ideas:
-Evaluate the blog entries and comments as they are updated. Also consider commenting on the students' blogs yourself as part of the ongoing dialogue.

Day 4 - Reading Assignment

Read all of Act IV.

Common Core Objectives

- CCSS.ELA-Literacy.CCRA.R.1
- CCSS.ELA-Literacy.CCRA.R.7
- CCSS.ELA-Literacy.CCRA.R.4
- CCSS.ELA-Literacy.CCRA.SL.6

Note that it is perfectly fine to expand any day's work into two days depending on the characteristics of the class, particularly if the class will engage in all of the suggested classroom exercises and activities and discuss all of the thought questions.

Content Summary for Teachers

Act IV, Scene i:

Iago and Othello continue to talk about the handkerchief and Desdemona's alleged affair. Iago says he has heard Cassio talk of lying with Desdemona. When he hears this, Othello flies into a rage and then falls unconscious. When Cassio enters, Iago tells him that Othello is having an epileptic fit and that Cassio should leave and return shortly. Othello wakes up and Iago asks him to stand nearby, explaining that he plans to talk to Cassio about Desdemona; Othello will be able to see Cassio's facial expressions, though not hear their words. In reality, Iago questions Cassio about Bianca to elicit the responses he seeks, and Othello thinks that Cassio's smiles of affection are about Desdemona.

Bianca arrives with Desdemona's handkerchief, which she angrily gives back to Cassio, insisting that it belongs to another one of his lovers. Bianca then leaves and Cassio goes after her, but not before Iago asks if he can dine with the two of them that evening in order to speak with Cassio. Othello and Iago then debrief, with Iago spurring on Othello's paranoia. Othello is now sure that Desdemona and Cassio are having an affair. Iago encourages Othello to strangle Desdemona in their bed in order to punish her. Iago will handle Cassio himself.

Lodovico and Desdemona arrive; Lodovico has a letter from Venice requesting Othello's return. As he reads, Othello becomes enraged at Desdemona and strikes her, shocking Lodovico. Othello announces that he will be happy to return to Venice and Cassio will take his place. Lodovico notes that Othello does not seem like his even-tempered self, and questions Othello's health and sanity. Iago refuses to weigh in and tells Lodovico to observe Othello's actions for himself.

Act IV, Scene ii:

Othello questions Emilia about the relationship between Desdemona and Cassio. Emilia defends Desdemona's honor and brings Desdemona in to talk to Othello herself. Othello furiously demands that Desdemona swear to her own honesty and loyalty, which she does. He refuses to believe her and rages on, refusing to accuse her directly but calling her a strumpet and a whore. Emilia interrupts their arguing and Othello leaves.

Emilia tries to comfort Desdemona, who is disturbed and seeks insights from Iago about Othello's behavior. Emilia is incensed and insists that someone must have turned Othello against Desdemona, but Iago dismisses the idea and calls her a fool. On his way out, Iago meets Roderigo, who is unhappy because he has not seen any progress regarding the promise of Desdemona's affections. Iago insists that Roderigo will have Desdemona soon, once Cassio has been killed. Roderigo accepts this temporarily, but wants to see results.

Act IV, Scene iii: After dinner, Othello sends Desdemona to bed and tells her to dismiss Emilia. Not wanting to incite his wrath, Desdemona tells Emilia to leave, but Emilia expresses concern about Othello's temper and Desdemona's safety. Desdemona seems to know that Othello will kill her; she sings a song about a woman who dies similarly, and resigns herself to her fate.

Thought Questions (students consider while they read)

1. Think about the Iago's use of imitation or echoing when he speaks to Othello. How is this changing in Act IV?
2. What do you notice about the meter of Othello's speech in this act?
3. How does Othello demonstrate that he is conflicted about Desdemona?
4. Why do you think Desdemona accepts her fate so easily? What else could she have done?
5. How does Othello's behavior in this act conform to the prejudiced expectations set out for him by his society?

Vocabulary (in order of appearance)

IV.i.27:

- Dotage: Old age, when one is weak

IV.i.47:

- Reproach: Disapproval or censure

IV.i.114:

- Importune: To plead with someone repeatedly

IV.i.194:

- Iniquity: Immoral behavior

IV.ii.16:

- Requite: To reciprocate, often in the sense of revenge

IV.ii.91:

- Cunning: Clever, often in a manipulative way

IV.ii.116:

- Chiding: Scolding

IV.ii.164:

- Abhor: To hate

Additional Homework

1. Try to imagine Desdemona's feelings as she speaks with her friend Emilia and anticipates her visit from Othello. Write a journal entry from her point of view.

Day 4 - Discussion of Thought Questions

1. Think about the Iago's use of imitation or echoing when he speaks to Othello. How is this changing in Act IV?

   Time: 7-10 min

   Discussion: In previous acts, Iago often echoed Othello rather than providing him with a direct answer (see, for instance, Act III, Scene iii). As Act IV begins, Othello is echoing Iago, perhaps because he is now more thoroughly under Iago's influence. Repeating Othello's own words back to him has been a subtle way for Iago to make Othello question his own sanity and influence Othello's conclusions.

2. What do you notice about the meter of Othello's speech in this act?

   Time: 5-7 min

   Discussion: Othello begins to speak in prose, rather than in verse, as he slips into violence and anger. His speech has been praised as one of his greatest virtues, but as he is driven insane by Iago and by his belief that Desdemona has been unfaithful, Othello begins to lose this quality.

3. How does Othello demonstrate that he is conflicted about Desdemona?

   Time: 5-7 min

   Discussion: During his conversations with Iago, Othello calls Desdemona good and kind and sweet one moment, and speaks quite violently about her the next. He also says that he fears confronting her because her "body and beauty" will prevent him from thinking clearly.

4. Why do you think Desdemona accepts her fate so easily? What else could she have done?

Time: 5-7 min

Discussion: Desdemona has shown herself to be endlessly loyal to Othello, so perhaps she thinks this is her wifely duty. Contemporary research shows it is common for victims of abuse to believe that they "deserve" what they are getting, so perhaps there is an element of that in Desdemona. Furthermore, she might not have much recourse as a woman, although as a noblewoman she has more leverage than others might.

5. How does Othello's behavior in this act conform to the prejudiced expectations set out for him by his society?

Time: 7-10 min

Discussion: Othello becomes violent, vengeful, and downright bestial as the play goes on. He compares himself to horned animals, strikes his wife, yells at her in public and in private, and generally becomes savage. These are precisely the qualities unfairly ascribed to his people based on race.

Day 4 - Short Answer Quiz

1. What does Iago tell Othello to do to Desdemona?

_____

2. What does the letter from Venice say?

_____

3. What does Othello do that shocks Lodovico?

_____

4. Why is Roderigo unhappy with Iago?

_____

5. What does Desdemona sing about?

_____

6. What does Bianca return to Cassio and why?

_____

7. What does Iago tell Cassio about Othello's fainting?

_____

8. What instructions does Desdemona give regarding her bed?

_____

9. Is Desdemona aware of Othello's plans to kill her?

_____

10. What does Emilia say when questioned about Desdemona's loyalty?

_____

Short Answer Quiz Key

1. He advises Othello to kill her, specifically by strangling her.
2. The Venetian army has called Othello back to Venice.
3. He hits Desdemona in front of everyone. (Othello's general harsh tone and agitated demeanor also shock Lodovico.)
4. Iago promised to win over Desdemona for Roderigo, and so far there has been no apparent progress.
5. She sings a sad song about false love and betrayal.
6. She returns Desdemona's handkerchief because she is convinced that it is from another woman.
7. He says that it is an epileptic fit.
8. She wants it to be made up with her wedding sheets.
9. Yes, she seems to be aware and to resign herself to her fate.
10. Emilia vouches for Desdemona's loyalty and says she has never observed anything untoward between Cassio and Desdemona.

Day 4 - Crossword Puzzle

ACROSS

3. Disapproval
6. _____ is unhappy with Iago.
8. Desdemona sings a song about a _____.
10. In public, Othello does this to Desdemona
13. Othello sends Desdemona to ____.
15. To plead repeatedly
17. To reciprocate
18. Iago and Cassio talk about his mistress _____.'
19. Old age
20. Othello ____ while talking to Iago.

DOWN

1. Desdemona wants her bed made with her ____ sheets.
2. Othello plans to ____ Desdemona.
4. Iago continues to ____ Othello.
5. To hate
7. Othello is asked to return to _____.
9. ____ plans to have Cassio killed.
11. Immoral behavior
12. Clever in a manipulative way
14. Othello tells Desdemona to ____ Emilia.
16. ____ defends Desdemona's honor.

Crossword Puzzle Answer Key

ACROSS

3. Disapproval
6. _____ is unhappy with Iago.
8. Desdemona sings a song about a _____.
10. In public, Othello does this to Desdemona
13. Othello sends Desdemona to ____.
15. To plead repeatedly
17. To reciprocate
18. Iago and Cassio talk about his mistress _____.
19. Old age
20. Othello ____ while talking to Iago.

DOWN

1. Desdemona wants her bed made with her _____ sheets.
2. Othello plans to ____ Desdemona.
4. Iago continues to _____ Othello.
5. To hate
7. Othello is asked to return to _____.
9. ____ plans to have Cassio killed.
11. Immoral behavior
12. Clever in a manipulative way
14. Othello tells Desdemona to _____ Emilia.
16. ____ defends Desdemona's honor.

Day 4 - Vocabulary Quiz

Terms

1. ____ Dotage
2. ____ Requite
3. ____ Importune
4. ____ Abhor
5. ____ Cunning
6. ____ Iniquity
7. ____ Reproach
8. ____ Chiding

Answers

A. Scolding
B. Clever, often in a manipulative way
C. To reciprocate, often in the sense of revenge
D. Disapproval or censure
E. To plead with someone repeatedly
F. Immoral behavior
G. Old age, when one is weak
H. To hate

Vocabulary Quiz Answer Key

1. G
2. C
3. E
4. H
5. B
6. F
7. D
8. A

Day 4 - Classroom Activities

1. Race, Gender and Culture in *Othello*

Kind of Activity: Research
Objective: To provide historical and cultural context for the play.
Common Core State Standards: CCSS.ELA-Literacy.CCRA.R.1 ;
CCSS.ELA-Literacy.CCRA.R.7
Time: 30 min

Structure:

In this activity, students will rotate among several stations (4-5 or more, depending on the time available), each of which will be set up with a document, video clip, interactive website, or other tool for learning about the culture and history of Elizabethan England, focusing particularly on issues of gender and race. At each station, provide worksheets with tools for analyzing the material presented. These can include thought questions, graphic organizers, space to respond artistically, and other tools. After everyone has visited all of the stations, have the students come together to discuss their impressions.

Stations might include:

-Race in Shakespeare: Relevant excerpts from Shakespeare's sonnets that touch on race, and/or critical essays on the subject

-Elizabethan Music: Audio recordings of Elizabethan music (along with lyrics and explanations, such as the information found here:
http://www.elizabethan-era.org.uk/elizabethan-music.htm)

-The Age of Exploration: Excerpts from travelogues of European explorers of the time

-Marriage in Elizabethan England: Excerpts from "A Discourse on Marriage and Wiving," written by Alexander Niccholes in 1615
(http://www.folger.edu/documents/STC%2018514Discourse%20of%20marriage%20

-Cultural Overview: A basic overview of the culture informing *Othello* (such as http://www.shakespearetheatre.org/plays/articles.aspx?&id=83)

Ideans for Differentiated Instruction:

-Provide materials of various lengths and complexities at each station, so that students can choose material that is appropriate for their skill level.

-Varying the stations available to include video, audio, written documents, and hands-on activities will provide options for students whose learning styles may differ.

-Circulate around the room to assist students who might need more scaffolding questions or other tools to navigate the materials provided.

Assessment Ideas:

-Have students submit their completed worksheets for assessment after visiting each of the stations.

-Assess student comprehension and analysis via participation in class discussion and responses to questions from the instructor and peers.

2. Willow Song

Kind of Activity: Performance
Objective: To help students understand the role of song in Shakespeare and other drama.
Common Core State Standards: CCSS.ELA-Literacy.CCRA.R.4 ; CCSS.ELA-Literacy.CCRA.SL.6
Time: 40 min

Structure:

Begin by asking students to recall any plays or films they have seen that feature songs or music performed by the characters (including other Shakespeare plays). Discuss their examples and how the music in each work contributed to the mood, character development, story, etc. Next, turn the students' attention to Desdemona's "Willow Song" in Act IV Scene iii. What role might it serve?

Break the students into small groups. Each group will prepare a dramatization of Desdemona's song and perform it for the class. They can create a tune for the song, set it to an existing tune, recite it all together, or choose another way to present it, as long as they can justify their choices. After the groups have had time to develop their songs and perform them, lead a discussion about what students discovered throughout the process: How did each group's interpretation differ? What were the commonalities? What can be gleaned about the role of the song in the play?

Ideans for Differentiated Instruction: -Students working in groups should share responsibilities according to their individual interests, talents, and skill levels.

Assessment Ideas:

-Assess the students' performances in terms of how well they demonstrate an appropriate level of analysis and understanding.

-Evaluate how well students contribute to the post-performance discussion.

Day 5 - Reading Assignment

Read all of Act V.

Common Core Objectives

- CCSS.ELA-Literacy.CCRA.R.6
- CCSS.ELA-Literacy.CCRA.R.9
- CCSS.ELA-Literacy.CCRA.W.3
- CCSS.ELA-Literacy.CCRA.W.9

Note that it is perfectly fine to expand any day's work into two days depending on the characteristics of the class, particularly if the class will engage in all of the suggested classroom exercises and activities and discuss all of the thought questions.

Content Summary for Teachers

Act V, Scene i:

Roderigo is waiting, at Iago's urging, to duel with Cassio. As far as Iago is concerned, it would be preferable if Roderigo and Cassio killed each other so that Iago's machinations remain secret. Cassio and Roderigo duel and are both injured. Othello hears the fight and arrives to find Cassio badly wounded. This pleases Othello and he leaves promptly.

Lodovico and Gratanio, and later Bianca and Emilia, also happen upon the duelers. Iago arrives as well and pretends not to know anything about the fight. Roderigo dies and Cassio is carried off to have his wounds dressed.

Act V, Scene ii:

Othello enters Desdemona's bedroom to find her asleep. He talks about how beautiful she looks but remains committed to murdering her. Desdemona wakes up and tries to convince Othello that she has been faithful to him, but he will have none of it and smothers her nearly to death. Emilia comes to the door and informs Othello that Roderigo has died but Cassio is still alive. Before she dies, Desdemona calls her death "guiltless," claiming that she has committed suicide. But Othello confesses the truth to Emilia, and recounts to her Iago's role in "uncovering" the "affair." Emilia is shocked and lashes out at Othello, screaming and crying out.

Gratiano, Montano, and Iago hear Emilia's screams and come to the bedroom. Iago's schemes are revealed and Othello is heartbroken. Iago stabs Emilia; as she dies, he is led out by officers. When they return with Iago, Othello stabs him. Cassio is brought in and Othello asks for his forgiveness now that he knows the truth. Othello then tells everyone to remember him as he is, and then kills himself. Cassio is temporarily instated as the leader of the Venetian troops in Cyprus. Iago's crimes will be tried in Venice.

Thought Questions (students consider while they read)

1. What role does Iago play in the duel between Cassio and Roderigo?
2. How does Iago connect with the audience (in V.i in particular, but also throughout the play)?
3. How does Othello evoke the symbols of light and dark when he speaks to Desdemona on her deathbed?
4. Does Othello's style of speaking change in his final scenes? How does it compare to his outbursts from Act III?
5. Why does Othello ask Desdemona if she has prayed?

Vocabulary (in order of appearance)

V.i.2:

- Rapier: A kind of sword

V.i.94:

- Palate: One's appreciation for tastes and flavors

V.i.23:

- Gait: One's manner of walking

V.i.117:

- Supped: Ate, had dinner

V.i.121:

- Strumpet: Whore

V.ii.5:

- Alabaster: A smooth white stone often used for decorative carvings

V.ii.45:

- Portents: Omens or signs

V.ii.51:

- Perjury: The act of lying under oath

V.ii.131:

- Belie: Fail to show the true nature of someone or something; betray

V.ii.151:

- Pernicious: Causing harm gradually

V.ii.211:

- Amorous: Related to love

V.ii.280:

- Rash: Hasty, careless

V.ii.299:

- Ensnared: Trapped

Additional Homework

1. Choose a major symbol from the play and write a paragraph or two about its importance and how it evolves, if at all, throughout the work.

Day 5 - Discussion of Thought Questions

1. What role does Iago play in the duel between Cassio and Roderigo?

   Time: 5-7 min

   Discussion: Iago instigates the duel and then makes sure that both men are wounded. He leaves, pretends to know nothing about the fight, and even wounds both Cassio and Roderigo himself, from behind so that he won't be noticed. Iago takes on the same role in this physical altercation as he has in the emotional entanglements throughout the play.

2. How does Iago connect with the audience (in V.i in particular, but also throughout the play)?

   Time: 5-7 min

   Discussion: Iago deceives both Roderigo and Cassio during their duel, sneaking around and lying about whose side he is on while wanting both men dead. He is honest only with the audience, confiding all of his plans and desires. This is true throughout the play: the audience alone knows Iago's true intentions and sees his schemes play out in their entirety. In this way, although Othello is the title character, Iago connects with the audience perhaps more than any other character.

3. How does Othello evoke the symbols of light and dark when he speaks to Desdemona on her deathbed?

   Time: 7-10 min

   Discussion: Othello focuses heavily on the whiteness of Desdemona's skin, and contrasts it with the darkness and evil of her soul. He also compares this metaphorical darkness with the color of his own skin; even Othello cannot escape these ingrained ideas about race and skin color. He has internalized these metaphors and seems fixated on them as he kills Desdemona.

4. Does Othello's style of speaking change in his final scenes? How does it compare to his outbursts from Act III?

Time: 5-7 min

Discussion: Othello returns to his metered, poetic style of speech in the last act. Although he has obviously not returned to sanity, he has regained some sense of composure, perhaps because he feels he has taken control of the situation. It's also possible that poetic language is a way to ignore the savagery of the acts he is committing, and a way to avoid having to reconcile his love for Desdemona with his brutality.

5. Why does Othello ask Desdemona if she has prayed?

Time: 7-10 min

Discussion: There are several ways to read this. Othello could be taunting Desdemona with her impending death, asking her if she has prayed as a way of implying that he plans to murder her. He shortly becomes more direct about this, but it's possible that his initial question is simply a cruel one. A more likely reading, though, is that he is showing her a kind of mercy, not wanting her to die without having repented for her sins.

Day 5 - Short Answer Quiz

1. Who orchestrates the duel between Roderigo and Cassio?

_____

2. What is Iago's fate at the end of the play?

_____

3. How does Emilia die?

_____

4. What does Othello ask Desdemona to do before he kills her?

_____

5. What does Desdemona say as she is dying?

_____

6. Who reveals Iago's schemes to Othello?

_____

7. What do we learn has happened to Brabantio (Desdemona's father)?

_____

8. How does Othello die?

_____

9. Who will lead the troops at Cyprus with Othello dead?

_____

10. What does Othello ask of Cassio before killing himself?

_____

Short Answer Quiz Key

1. Iago.
2. Iago will be tried for his crimes in Venice.
3. Iago stabs her.
4. He asks her to pray and repent for her sins.
5. She calls her death "guiltless" and says that she brought it on herself.
6. Emilia.
7. He has died.
8. He kills himself.
9. Cassio.
10. He asks Cassio to forgive him.

Day 5 - Crossword Puzzle

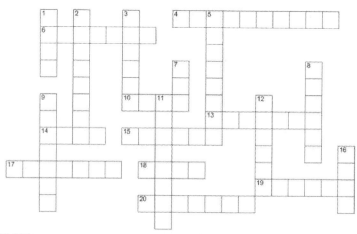

ACROSS

4. Causing harm gradually
6. Related to love
10. Brabantio has _____.
13. Cassio will be the new _____.
14. Hasty or careless
15. _____ will lead the troops at Cyprus.
17. Othello commits this act.
18. Othello stabs _____.
19. _____ interrupts Desdemona's murder.
20. Lying under oath

DOWN

1. One's manner of walking
2. Omens
3. Dined
5. _____ is killed during a duel.
7. Desdemona dies in her _____.
8. Iago stabs _____ to death.
9. Othello asks Cassio to _____ him.
11. Trapped
12. Where Iago will stand trial.
16. Othello asks Desdemona to _____.

Crossword Puzzle Answer Key

ACROSS
4. Causing harm gradually
6. Related to love
10. Brabantio has _____.
13. Cassio will be the new _____.
14. Hasty or careless
15. ___ will lead the troops at Cyprus.
17. Othello commits this act.
18. Othello stabs _____.
19. _____ interrupts Desdemona's murder.
20. Lying under oath

DOWN
1. One's manner of walking
2. Omens
3. Dined
5. _____ is killed during a duel.
7. Desdemona dies in her ____.
8. Iago stabs _____ to death.
9. Othello asks Cassio to _____ him.
11. Trapped
12. Where Iago will stand trial.
16. Othello asks Desdemona to _____.

Day 5 - Vocabulary Quiz

Terms

1. ____ Supped
2. ____ Belie
3. ____ Portents
4. ____ Pernicious
5. ____ Rash
6. ____ Gait
7. ____ Rapier
8. ____ Amorous
9. ____ Strumpet
10. ____ Alabaster

Answers

A. A kind of sword
B. Causing harm gradually
C. Dined
D. Omens
E. Whore
F. A smooth white stone often used for decorative carvings
G. Related to love
H. Hasty, careless
I. Fail to show the true nature of someone or something; betray
J. One's manner of walking

Vocabulary Quiz Answer Key

1. C
2. I
3. D
4. B
5. H
6. J
7. A
8. G
9. E
10. F

Day 5 - Classroom Activities

1. *Othello* in Film

Kind of Activity: Classwide Discussion
Objective: To explore modern adaptations of the Othello story
Common Core State Standards: CCSS.ELA-Literacy.CCRA.R.9 ;
CCSS.ELA-Literacy.CCRA.R.6
Time: Length of film(s) plus an additional 20 minutes

Structure:

Screen a modern film adaptation of *Othello*, or perhaps segments from
several adaptations. Try to include traditional presentations of the story as
well as modernized versions, such as 2001's *O* or the 1997 film *Kaliyattam*,
which sets the story in India.

Questions for discussion after the film(s) might include:

-What is effective about these adaptations? What doesn't work as well?

-If you had the chance to adapt *Othello*, what medium do you think would
be best and why?

-What aspects would you handle differently than the versions we've seen?

-How do the modern adaptations handle race? How relevant is this story to
modern viewers, in terms of race issues?

Have students select a key scene of their choice, and watch the presentation
of this moment in several of the adaptations. Discuss the difference and
similarities in how the same moment was expressed. What elements are
maintained in all versions? How are all the versions different? Which is the
most effective? Which is the most conservative?

Ideans for Differentiated Instruction:

-Choose a variety of adaptations to screen, which will help to engage
students with different tastes, learning styles, and cultural backgrounds.

-Encourage students to read along in their texts if they are having trouble
following the film.

Assessment Ideas:
-Assess the students' understanding of and engagement with the material

based on their contributions to the classwide discussion.

2. Alternate Endings

Kind of Activity: Collaborative Writing
Objective: To imagine other possible endings for the play.
Common Core State Standards: CCSS.ELA-Literacy.CCRA.W.3 ;
CCSS.ELA-Literacy.CCRA.W.9
Time: 40 min

Structure:

Briefly review the events of Act V together. Ask the students to think about what they liked and did not like about the play's final act, and then give them an opportunity to re-imagine a key scene from it. For example, perhaps they feel Desdemona should have resisted Othello more vehemently; perhaps they think it would have been interesting if Cassio had died and Othello had no chance to ask for forgiveness.

Break the students into small groups. Each group will work together to write an alternate version of a scene or moment from Act V. They might choose to stay within the medium of drama, but that shouldn't be a requirement; the final product might be a prose piece, an artistic rendering, or another format altogether.

After giving them time to write and brainstorm, ask a representative from each group to summarize their alternate scene. Encourage the rest of the class to ask questions, which might include: Why did you reject this scene as written? Why did you choose to rewrite it in this way?

Ideans for Differentiated Instruction:

-Brainstorm ideas for alternate endings before asking the students to produce their own from scratch.

-Provide scaffolding questions both for the writing process and for the discussion process.

-Allow students to complete the activity in whatever medium they think is the best fit, based on what resources are available.

Assessment Ideas:
-Have students turn in their work for evaluation by the instructor, in addition to discussing it with the class.

Final Paper

Essay Questions

1. Examine the power of storytelling and speech in *Othello*. Who possess these powers, how do they use them, and how does that change throughout the play?

2. Emilia says in Act IV Scene iii, "Let husbands know / Their wives have sense like them: / they see, and smell, / And have their palates for both sweet and sour / As husbands have" (92-95). Is this a central problem for the men of the play? Why or why not?

3. How is Othello's murder of Desdemona atypical for a Shakespearian tragedy?

4. Compare Iago to a villain from another play or novel. Iago's motivations are often opaque; what about those of this other villain? How are their tactics similar and where do they diverge? What do these comparisons reveal about Iago?

5. Is Othello a classical tragic hero? Why or why not?

6. Choose one of the play's recurring symbols (e.g. blackness and whiteness, the handkerchief, animal imagery) and trace its development throughout the play.

Advice on research sources

A. School or community library

Ask your reference librarian for help locating books on the following subjects:

* Shakespeare

* Elizabethan England

* Marriage in Renaissance Europe

* Dramatic representations of betrayal and jealousy

* Dramatic representations of madness

B. Personal Experience

Have you ever felt like an outsider, perhaps despite achieving a prominent position in a social group? Have you ever felt betrayed? Have you ever deceived someone for personal gain?

Grading rubric for essays

Style:

* Words: spelling and diction

* Sentences: grammar and punctuation

* Paragraphs: organization

* Essay: structure

* Argument: rhetoric, reasonableness, creativity

Content:

* Accuracy

* Use of evidence

* Addressing the question

* Completeness

* Use of literary concepts

* Addressing complex and sensitive subjects with understanding and nuance

Final Paper Answer Key

Remember that essays about literature should not be graded with a cookie-cutter approach whereby specific words or ideas are required. See the grading rubric above for a variety of criteria to use in assessing answers to the essay questions. This answer key thus functions as a store of ideas for students who need additional guidance in framing their answers.

1. Examine the power of storytelling and speech in *Othello*. Who possess these powers, how do they use them, and how does that change throughout the play?

   Othello is introduced as an educated, well-spoken man; he has won over both Desdemona and Brabantio with his storytelling and makes his case eloquently to the council of senators in the first act. Strong responses will note the importance of Othello's fluidity with speech in the context of his outsider status. It is also important to note Iago's storytelling abilities, as it is his ability to spin a web of complex lies that drives the entire action of the play. Othello's powers of language are not enough to help him avoid Iago's influence, as we can see in the marked changes that come to Othello's style of speech and manner when he is driven mad by Iago's lies.

2. Emilia says in Act IV Scene iii, "Let husbands know / Their wives have sense like them: / they see, and smell, / And have their palates for both sweet and sour / As husbands have" (92-95). Is this a central problem for the men of the play? Why or why not?

   Strong answers will discuss Othello's apparent difficulties with trusting his wife or having a direct conversation with her as an equal about Iago's allegations (arguably a product of the era, but still a detriment to their marriage). Responses might also note Iago's general inability to empathize, not only with Emilia or with women—he appears to simply enjoy manipulating and deceiving people, so for him it is less important whether or not wives have the same emotional depths as men do.

3. How is Othello's murder of Desdemona atypical for a Shakespearian tragedy?

   Othello shows a strange kind of mercy and remorse even as he kills Desdemona. The two talk at length about her impending death, and Othello expresses genuine concern about whether she has prayed so that she will die having repented for her sins. Othello praises Desdemona's beauty and her apparent innocence despite remaining resolved to kill her. A strong response might argue that it is difficult for Othello to murder Desdemona in cold blood because he loves her, and the intimacy and strangeness of the scene is a reflection of those opposing forces.

4. Compare Iago to a villain from another play or novel. Iago's motivations are often opaque; what about those of this other villain? How are their tactics similar and where do they diverge? What do these comparisons reveal about Iago?

Individual responses will depend on what other text is chosen for comparison, but strong essays might note that Iago is a rather two-dimensional villain, seeming to revel in his own cruelty and deception without much reason given for his actions. His methods as a villain are also interesting, in that they revolve largely around telling lies and convincing other people to do things—he rarely gets his own hands dirty. Choosing a text whose villain is more hands-on might provide for a rich essay comparing the two.

5. Is Othello a classical tragic hero? Why or why not?

Strong responses will note that Othello certainly has a tragic flaw, in that he is excessively prideful about his reputation (a concern perhaps borne of the racial prejudice he experiences). Although he may not be of noble birth, he has risen to the rank of general and is well-educated and respected. The play is unmistakably about his tragic fall, and he sacrifices himself although it is too late to save those around him.

6. Choose one of the play's recurring symbols (e.g. blackness and whiteness, the handkerchief, animal imagery) and trace its development throughout the play.

Answers will vary depending on which symbol the student chooses. For instance, an essay about the symbolism of blackness and whiteness should include a discussion of race, particularly Desdemona's whiteness and Othello's blackness. This comes up immediately in the play when the couple elopes and Venice is scandalized at their interracial relationship. Desdemona, pure and loyal and good, is white, and this is much remarked upon by many characters, including Othello. Othello is also quite aware of his race and the negative cultural associations with his blackness. Light and darkness are also important outside of race here, but the racial component is always underlying references to this symbol.

Final Exam

A. Multiple Choice

Circle the letter corresponding to the best answer.

1. Desdemona's father

    (A) Gratanio
    (B) Roderigo
    (C) Brabantio
    (D) Cassio

2. The play is set mostly in _____.

    (A) Troy
    (B) Syracuse
    (C) Cyprus
    (D) Venice

3. Who is Othello's ensign?

    (A) Roderigo
    (B) Brabantio
    (C) Iago
    (D) Cassio

4. How does Desdemona die?

    (A) She dies of cholera.
    (B) Cassio kills her.
    (C) She dies in childbirth.
    (D) Othello kills her.

5. How do the other characters describe Iago?

    (A) Honest and loyal
    (B) Angry and sullen
    (C) Withdrawn and intimidating
    (D) Hardworking and narrowminded

6. What is Othello accused of in the first act?

   (A) Using magic to woo Desdemona.
   (B) He is not accused of anything.
   (C) Treason against the state.
   (D) Killing a fellow officer.

7. The Venetians are at war with whom?

   (A) The Greeks
   (B) The Phoenicians
   (C) The Spanish
   (D) The Turks

8. What is Othello's ancestry?

   (A) He is Venetian
   (B) He is a Moor
   (C) He is English
   (D) He is a Turk

9. Who is Iago's wife?

   (A) Desdemona
   (B) Bianca
   (C) Emilia
   (D) Flavia

10. Why does Othello fire Cassio?

   (A) Iago tells him to.
   (B) Cassio has been having an affair with Desdemona.
   (C) Cassio has not been performing his duties well.
   (D) Cassio was involved in a drunken fight while on night watch.

11. Iago provokes a duel between whom?

   (A) Cassio and Montano
   (B) Roderigo and Cassio
   (C) Himself and Othello
   (D) Roderigo and Desdemona

12. Who offers to advocate for Cassio with Othello?

   (A) Roderigo
   (B) Desdemona
   (C) Brabantio
   (D) Emilia

13. What object does Desdemona lose?

   (A) Her handkerchief
   (B) Her brooch
   (C) Her keys
   (D) Her hat

14. What is Iago's fate?

   (A) He is to return to Venice for trial
   (B) He is to marry Desdemonia
   (C) He is promoted to General
   (D) He dies at the end of the play

15. How does Emilia die?

   (A) She dies in childbirth
   (B) She kills herself
   (C) Othello kills her
   (D) Iago kills her

16. What does Iago ask Emilia to steal from Desdemona?

    (A) Her handkerchief
    (B) Her brooch
    (C) Her earrings
    (D) Her hat

17. What does Iago promise Roderigo?

    (A) That Bianca will fall in love with him
    (B) That Roderigo will be promoted to General
    (C) That Roderigo will become rich
    (D) That Desdemona will fall in love with him

18. Who is Cassio's mistress?

    (A) Kalliope
    (B) Catherine
    (C) Bianca
    (D) Emilia

19. Who survives the duel that Iago instigates?

    (A) Gratanio
    (B) Roderigo
    (C) No one
    (D) Cassio

20. What animal is Othello compared to?

    (A) A bird
    (B) A fish
    (C) A lizard
    (D) A ram

B. Short Answer

1. What reasons does Iago give for his actions?

_____

2. What prevents the Turkish fleet from reaching Cyprus?

_____

3. What is Cassio's weakness, which Iago exploits?

_____

4. How does Iago suggest Cassio gain Othello's favor?

_____

5. What is the significance of Desdemona's handkerchief?

_____

6. Who does Iago try to imply is responsible for Cassio's injuries?

_____

7. What does Iago hope will happen when Roderigo attacks Cassio?

_____

8. How does Othello show mercy to Desdemona?

_____

9. What leads Iago to kill Emilia?

_____

10. What does Othello ask of those gathered before he kills himself?

_____

C. Vocabulary

Terms   Answers

1. ____ Portents   A. Omens or signs
2. ____ Rash   B. Passionate or forceful
3. ____ Surfeited   C. Disapproval or censure
4. ____ Relish   D. Overly full or satiated
5. ____ Prating   E. Charity
6. ____ Vehement   F. Made holy, consecrated
7. ____ Hallowed   G. Talking inanely and at length
8. ____ Alms   H. Appreciate or savor
9. ____ Cunning   I. Hasty or careless
10. ____ Reproach   J. Clever, often in a manipulative way

D. Short Essays

1. Is there a moral to *Othello*? If so, what is it and how is it revealed?

_____

_____

_____

_____

2. How is animal imagery used throughout the play?

_____

_____

_____

_____

3. What is the role of dramatic irony in *Othello*?

_____

_____

_____

_____

D. Short Essays

Final Exam Answer Key

A. Multiple Choice Answer Key

1. C
2. C
3. C
4. D
5. A
6. A
7. D
8. B
9. C
10. D
11. B
12. B
13. A
14. A
15. D
16. A
17. D
18. C
19. D
20. D

B. Short Answer Key

1. He is unhappy that he has been passed over for a promotion, and he suspects that Othello has slept with Iago's wife Emilia.
2. A storm.
3. He has trouble moderating his alcohol consumption.
4. Iago tells him to appeal to Desdemona, who will influence Othello's decision about Cassio.
5. Othello gave the handkerchief to Desdemona as a gift, and it becomes a central piece of Iago's plot to implicate Cassio and Desdemona in an affair.
6. He implicates Bianca.
7. He hopes that they will kill each other so that neither can reveal Iago's deceptions.
8. He asks her to pray before he kills her.

9. Emilia has revealed all of Iago's plots to Othello and the others.
10. He asks them to remember him as he is now.

C. Vocabulary Answer Key

1. A
2. I
3. D
4. H
5. G
6. B
7. F
8. E
9. J
10. C

D. Short Essays Answer Key

1. Strong responses might identify a warning against jealousy or deception, as those qualities cause the chaos and disaster that characterize the play. Iago's deceptions and Othello's jealousy run rampant and ruin the lives of nearly every character in the play. Another possible moral is the importance of trust and self-knowledge: Iago is able to prey upon Othello partly because Othello is so concerned with his reputation and does not pay enough attention to his inner life and his relationship with Desdemona.
2. A strong essay will note two main uses of animalistic imagery: first, Othello is frequently compared to an animal (usually a bull) in the context of his sexual relationship with Desdemona. This serves as a way for Iago, Roderigo, and others to speak ill of the interracial relationship at the center of the play. Second, bestial imagery is invoked as Othello unravels; he becomes less human under Iago's influence, unable to articulate his thoughts and consumed with base emotions like jealousy and rage.
3. Responses should focus on the relationship between Iago and the audience. We alone know the truth of his intentions, and we alone see his entire plot unfold. This creates a connection between Iago and the audience, without which we might find the villain's actions uninteresting due to their apparent lack of motivation. Dramatic irony also creates anticipation and tension as the audience waits to see who will learn about Iago's schemes and how, and whether it will happen in time to save the characters and their relationships.

Lesson Plans

Getting you the grade since 1999™

Other Lesson Plans from GradeSaver™

1984
The Adventures of
   Huckleberry Finn
Animal Farm
Antigone
The Book Thief
Brave New World
The Canterbury Tales
The Crucible
Death of a Salesman
Emily Dickinson's
   Collected Poems
Fahrenheit 451
The Great Gatsby
Gulliver's Travels
Hamlet
Heart of Darkness
Into the Wild
The Kite Runner
Life of Pi
Lord of the Flies
Macbeth
MAUS
Oedipus Rex or Oedipus
   the King
Of Mice and Men
Othello
Poe's Poetry
The Road
The Scarlet Letter
A Streetcar Named
   Desire
To Kill a Mockingbird
The Yellow Wallpaper

For our full list of over 300 Study Guides, Quizzes, Lesson Plans
Sample College Application Essays, Literature Essays and E-texts, visit:

www.gradesaver.com